IT'S TIME TO EAT MAC AND CHEESE BITES

It's Time to Eat MAC AND CHEESE BITES

Walter the Educator

Silent King Books
A WhichHead Entertainment Imprint

Copyright © 2024 by Walter the Educator

All rights reserved. No part of this book may be reproduced in any manner whatsoever without written per- mission except in the case of brief quotations embodied in critical articles and reviews.

First Printing, 2024

Disclaimer

This book is a literary work; the story is not about specific persons, locations, situations, and/or circumstances unless mentioned in a historical context. Any resemblance to real persons, locations, situations, and/or circumstances is coincidental. This book is for entertainment and informational purposes only. The author and publisher offer this information without warranties expressed or implied. No matter the grounds, neither the author nor the publisher will be accountable for any losses, injuries, or other damages caused by the reader's use of this book. The use of this book acknowledges an understanding and acceptance of this disclaimer.

It's Time to Eat MAC AND CHEESE BITES is a collectible early learning book by Walter the Educator suitable for all ages belonging to Walter the Educator's Time to Eat Book Series. Collect more books at WaltertheEducator.com

USE THE EXTRA SPACE TO TAKE NOTES AND DOCUMENT YOUR MEMORIES

MAC AND CHEESE BITES

It's time to eat, oh, what a treat,

It's Time to Eat Mac and Cheese Bites

Mac and Cheese Bites, warm and neat.

Golden crust, so crisp, so round,

Cheesy joy that's best around!

They sit and sizzle on the plate,

Tiny treasures, can't be late!

One little bite, then two, then three,

Oh, how tasty they can be!

Dip them in ketchup, swirl them in sauce,

Every bite's a flavor boss.

Cheese so gooey, soft inside,

A snack that fills your heart with pride.

Mom says, "Slow down! Don't eat too fast!"

But they're so yummy, they never last.

Crunchy munchy bites so small,

I think I love them best of all!

It's Time to Eat Mac and Cheese Bites

"Share with me!" my sister calls,

But I'm too busy, mouth is full!

She grabs a bite; I smile and grin,

Mac and Cheese is meant to win.

The cheese is melty, oh, so creamy,

A dream come true, like something dreamy.

Every bite a little hug,

Warm and snug like a favorite rug.

Little hands grab one, then more,

Mac and Cheese Bites we all adore.

Friends come over; we share the plate,

A snack like this is worth the wait!

When the plate is empty, we all sigh,

Wipe the crumbs from lips and eyes.

"More, please!" echoes through the room,

It's Time to Eat Mac and Cheese Bites

Mac and Cheese Bites chase away the gloom.

So next time hunger comes to play,

Let Mac and Cheese Bites save the day!

They're fun to eat, they bring delight,

A perfect snack both day and night!

When dinner's done and plates are clean,

We dream of bites in golden sheen.

"Tomorrow, more!" we cheer with glee,

It's Time to Eat Mac and Cheese Bites

Mac and Cheese Bites, wait for me!

ABOUT THE CREATOR

Walter the Educator is one of the pseudonyms for Walter Anderson. Formally educated in Chemistry, Business, and Education, he is an educator, an author, a diverse entrepreneur, and he is the son of a disabled war veteran. "Walter the Educator" shares his time between educating and creating. He holds interests and owns several creative projects that entertain, enlighten, enhance, and educate, hoping to inspire and motivate you. Follow, find new works, and stay up to date with Walter the Educator™

at WaltertheEducator.com

www.ingramcontent.com/pod-product-compliance
Lightning Source LLC
LaVergne TN
LVHW010623070526
838199LV00063BA/5255